BUTTERFLIES

Common Morpho
Morpho peleides
To 5 in. (13 cm)
Brilliant iridescent blue butterfly.

Giant Owl
Caligo memnon
To 6 in. (15 cm)

Malachite
Siproeta stelenes
To 3 in. (8 cm)

Sapho Longwing
Heliconius sapho
To 3 in. (8 cm)

Ruby-spotted Swallowtail
Papilio anchisiades
To 5 in. (13 cm)

Thoas Swallowtail
Heraclides thoas
To 5 in. (13 cm)

Julia
Dryas iulia
To 3.5 in. (9 cm)

The Mosaic
Colobura dirce
To 3 in. (8 cm)

Pink Cattleheart
Parides iphidamas
To 5 in. (13 cm)

Passionflower Butterfly
Heliconius hecale zuleika
To 4 in. (10 cm)

Mexican Bluewing
Myscelia ethusa
To 3 in. (8 cm)

Gray Cracker
Hamadryas februa
To 2.5 in. (6 cm)

Zebra Longwing
Heliconius charithonia
To 3.5 in. (9 cm)

Isabella
Eueides isabella
To 3 in. (8 cm)

$7.95 U.S.
$9.95 CAN
ISBN 978-1-58355-867-6
50795
9 781583 558676
UPC 8 84682 01156 6
10987654321
Made in the USA

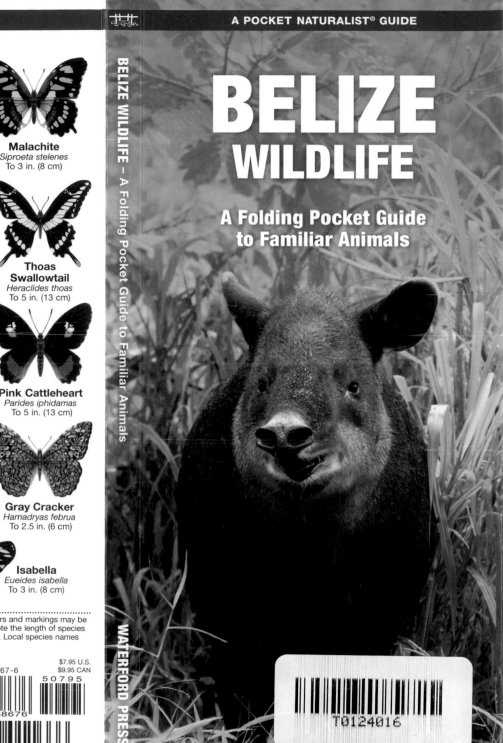

BELIZE WILDLIFE

A Folding Pocket Guide to Familiar Animals

BELIZE WILDLIFE – A Folding Pocket Guide to Familiar Animals

WATERFORD PRESS

T0124016

REPTILES & AMPHIBIANS

Marine Toad (Spring Chicken)
Rhinella marina
To 15 in. (38 cm)
Note huge size.

Gulf Coast Toad
Bufo valliceps
To 5 in. (13 cm)
Call is a short, repeated trill.

Red-eyed Leaf Frog
Agalychnis callidryas
To 3 in. (8 cm)
Note enlarged toe pads. One of 39 species of Costa Rican treefrog.

Loggerhead
Caretta caretta
To 4 ft. (1.2 m)
Shell is streamlined.

Mexican Treefrog
Smilisca baudini
To 2 in. (5 cm)
Note stripes on legs.

Green Sea Turtle
Chelonia mydas
To 5 ft. (1.5 m)

Central American River Turtle (Kickatee)
Dermatemys mawii
To 26 in. (65 cm)

Red-eared Slider
Trachemys scripta elegans
To 11 in. (28 cm)

Brown Anole
Anolis sargrei
To 9 in. (23 cm)
Introduced species.

Green Iguana (Bamboo Chicken)
Iguana iguana
To 5 ft. (1.5 m)

Yucatan Striped Gecko
Coleonyx elegans
To 6 in. (15 cm)

Spiny-tailed Iguana (Wish Willy)
Ctenosaura similis
To 5 ft. (1.5 m)

Striped Basilisk (Jesus Lizard)
Basiliscus vittatus
To 24 in. (60 cm)
Is able to "run" on top of the water for short distances when fleeing a predator.

Fer-de-lance (Yellow-jawed Tommygoff)
Bothrops asper
To 8 ft. (2.4 m)
Venomous.

REPTILES & AMPHIBIANS

Mayan Coral Snake
Micrurus hippocrepis
To 3 ft. (90 cm)
Venomous.

Boa Constrictor (Wowla)
Boa constrictor imperator
To 8 ft. (2.4 m)

Eyelash Viper
Bothriechis schlegelii To 30 in. (75 cm)
Has horn-like scales over each eye. Color is variable. Venomous.

Green Vine Snake
Oxybelis fulgidus To 6.5 ft. (2 m)

American Crocodile
Crocodylus acutus To 20 ft. (6 m)
Large, primarily coastal, saltwater species has a narrow, pointed snout.

Morelet's Crocodile
Crocodylus moreletii
To 14 ft. (4.2 m)
Freshwater species has a broad snout.

MAMMALS

Virginia Opossum
Didelphis virginiana
To 40 in. (1 m)

Water Opossum
Chironectes minimus
To 12 in. (30 cm)

Common Vampire Bat
Desmodus rotundus
To 4 in. (10 cm)
Feeds on the blood of animals.

Deppe's Squirrel
Sciurus deppei vivax
To 16 in. (40 cm)

Black Mastiff Bat
Molossus ater
To 8 in. (20 cm)
Large bat has a dog-like face.

Central American Agouti (Rabbit)
Dasyprocta puctata
To 20 in. (50 cm)

Long-tailed Weasel
Mustela frenata
To 21 in. (53 cm)

Paca (Gibnut)
Agouti paca
To 28 in. (70 cm)

MAMMALS

Neotropical Otter
Lontra longicaudis To 30 in. (75 cm)

Northern Tamandua (Antsbear)
Tamandua mexicana
To 32 in. (80 cm)
Eats primarily ants.

Grison
Galictis vittata To 22 in. (55 cm)

Kinkajou
Potos flavus
To 22 in. (55 cm)
The similar olingo is smaller and has a bushier tail.

Silky Anteater
Cyclopes didactylus
To 7 in. (18 cm)

Mexican Hairy Porcupine
Coendou mexicanus
To 16 in. (40 cm)

Striped Hog-nosed Skunk
Conepatus semistriatus
To 20 in. (50 cm)
One of 3 skunk species.

Southern Spotted Skunk
Spilogale angustifrons
To 22 in. (55 cm)

Tayra
Eira barbara To 28 in. (70 cm)
Large weasel-like mammal.

Giant Anteater
Myrmecophaga tridactyla
To 7 ft. (2.1 m)

Nine-banded Armadillo
Dasypus novemcinctus
To 32 in. (80 cm)

Common Raccoon
Procyon lotor To 40 in. (1 m)

White-nosed Coati
Nasua narica
To 52 in. (1.3 m)

Jaguar (Tiger)
Panthera onca To 8 ft. (2.4 m)
Coat is typically tan and spotted. Jaguars with all-black coats are called panthers.

MAMMALS

Jaguarundi
Puma yagouaroundi
To 30 in. (75 cm)
Coat is reddish to blackish.

Ocelot
Leopardus pardalis
To 4.5 ft. (1.35 m)

Margay
Leopardus wiedii
To 30 in. (75 cm)

Mountain Lion
Puma concolor
To 9 ft. (2.7 m)

Common Gray Fox
Urocyon cinereoargenteus
To 3.5 ft. (1 m)

Coyote
Canis latrans To 52 in. (1.3 m)

Central American Spider Monkey
Ateles geoffroyi
To 26 in. (65 cm)

Black Howler Monkey (Baboon)
Alouatta pigra
To 52 in. (1.3 m)
Roaring call is heard in the mornings and evenings.

Red Brocket Deer (Antelope)
Mazama americana
To 56 in. (1.4 m)
Note small horns.

Collared Peccary
Pecari tajacu
To 40 in. (1 m)

Baird's Tapir (Mountain Cow)
Tapirus bairdii
To 6.5 ft. (2 m)
Note long snout.

White-tailed Deer
Odocoileus virginianus
To 7 ft. (2.1 m)
Fluffy tail is white below and held aloft when running.

Queen Angelfish
Holacanthus ciliaris
To 12 in. (30 cm)

Blue Tang
Acanthurus coeruleus
To 14 in. (35 cm)

Spotfin Butterflyfish
Chaetodon ocellatus
To 8 in. (20 cm)

Blue-striped Grunt
Haemulon sciurus
To 16 in. (40 cm)

Spotted Eagle Ray
Aetobatus narinari
To 9 ft. (2.7 m)

Spadefish
Chaetodipterus faber
To 3 ft. (90 cm)

White Grunt
Haemulon plumierii
To 18 in. (45 cm)

Stingray
Hypanus americanus
To 5 ft. (1.5 m)
Thin, whip-like tail has one or more venomous spines.

Porkfish
Anisotremus virginicus
To 15 in. (38 cm)

Sergeant Major
Abudefduf saxatilis
To 8 in. (20 cm)

Smooth Trunkfish
Lactophrys triqueter
To 12 in. (30 cm)

Squirrelfish
Holocentrus adscensionis
To 12 in. (30 cm)

Bonefish
Albula vulpes To 3 ft. (90 cm)

Yellow Goatfish
Mulloidichthys martinicus To 15 in. (38 cm)

Lionfish
Pteois volitans
To 15 in. (38 cm)

Bluehead
Thalassoma bifasciatum To 5 in. (13 cm)

Queen Parrotfish
Scarus vetula To 20 in. (50 cm)

Queen Triggerfish
Balistes vetula
To 19 in. (48 cm)

Great Barracuda
Sphyraena barracuda To 6 ft. (1.8 m)
Has jutting lower jaw and prominent teeth.

Giant Porcupinefish
Diodon hystrix To 3 ft. (90 cm)
Body spines become raised when the fish inflates itself with water.

Spotted Moray Eel
Gymnothorax moringa
To 4 ft. (1.2 m)

Nurse Shark
Ginglymostoma cirratum To 18 ft. (5.4 m)
Bottom-dweller has two dorsal fins and prominent mouth whiskers (barbels).

Green Moray
Gymnothorax funebris
To 6 ft. (1.8 m)

Sungrebe
Heliornis fulica
To 12 in. (30 cm)

Neotropic Cormorant
Phalacrocorax brasilianus
To 26 in. (65 m)

Green Heron (Poor Joe)
Butorides virescens
To 22 in. (55 cm)

Great Blue Heron (Toby Full Pot)
Ardea herodias
To 4.5 ft. (1.4 m)

Magnificent Frigatebird
Fregata magnificens
To 40 in. (1 m)
Note huge wingspan.

Brown Pelican
Pelecanus occidentalis
To 50 in. (1.3 m)

Little Blue Heron
Egretta caerulea
To 2 ft. (60 cm)

Anhinga
Anhinga anhinga
To 3 ft. (90 cm)

Roseate Spoonbill
Platalea ajaja
To 32 in. (80 cm)
Bill is flattened at the tip.

Northern Jacana (Georgie Bull)
Jacana spinosa
To 10 in. (25 cm)

Jabiru (Turk)
Jabiru mycteria
To 55 in. (1.4 m)
Endangered.

Wood Stork (Turk)
Mycteria americana
To 4 ft. (1.2 m)
Dark head is naked.

White Ibis
Eudocimus albus
To 28 in. (70 cm)

Cattle Egret
Bubulcus ibis
To 20 in. (50 cm)

Snowy Egret
Egretta thula
To 26 in. (65 cm)
Note black bill and yellow feet.

Great Egret
Ardea alba
To 38 in. (95 cm)
Note yellow bill and black feet.

Lesser Yellow-headed Vulture
Cathartes burrovianus
To 26 in. (65 cm)

King Vulture
Sarcoramphus papa
To 32 in. (80 cm)

Turkey Vulture
Cathartes aura
To 32 in. (80 cm)
Note red head and two-toned underwings.

Osprey
Pandion haliaetus
To 2 ft. (60 cm)
Fish-eating raptor.

Black Vulture
Coragyps atratus
To 27 in. (68 cm)
Note gray wing tips.

Roadside Hawk
Buteo magnirostris
To 16 in. (40 cm)

Spectacled Owl
Pulsatrix perspicillata
To 18 in. (45 cm)

Red-lored Parrot
Amazona autumnalis
To 13 in. (33 cm)

Yellow-lored Parrot
Amazona xantholora
To 12 in. (30 cm)

White-fronted Parrot
Amazona albifrons
To 11 in. (28 cm)

Blue-fronted Parrot
Amazona aestiva
To 14 in. (35 cm)

Mealy Parrot
Amazona farinosa
To 16 in. (40 cm)
Note bluish crown.

White-crowned Parrot
Pionus senilis
To 10 in. (25 cm)

Squirrel Cuckoo
Piaya cayana
To 20 in. (50 cm)

Scarlet Macaw
Ara macao
To 34 in. (85 cm)

Keel-billed Toucan
Ramphastos sulfuratus
To 19 in. (48 cm)
National bird of Belize.

Collared Aracari
Pteroglossus torquatus
To 16 in. (40 cm)

Black-headed Trogon
Trogon melanocephalus
To 11 in. (28 cm)

Ringed Kingfisher
Megaceryle torquata
To 14 in. (35 cm)

Belted Kingfisher
Megaceryle alcyon
To 14 in. (35 cm)

Green Kingfisher
Chloroceryle americana
To 8 in. (20 cm)

Green-breasted Mango
Anthracothorax prevostii
To 5 in. (13 cm)

White-bellied Emerald
Amazilia candida
To 4.3 in. (11 cm)

Rufous-tailed Hummingbird
Amazilia tzacatl
To 4 in. (10 cm)

Cinnamon Hummingbird
Amazilia rutila
To 4 in. (10 cm)

Plain Chachalaca
Ortalis vetula
To 2 ft. (60 cm)

Yucatan Woodpecker
Melanerpes pygmaeus
To 8 in. (20 cm)

Great Curassow
Crax rubra
To 3 ft. (90 cm)

Fork-tailed Flycatcher
Tyrannus savana
To 16 in. (40 cm)

Great Kiskadee
Pitangus sulphuratus
To 9 in. (23 cm)

Tropical Kingbird
Tyrannus melancholicus
To 8 in. (20 cm)

Mangrove Swallow
Tachycineta albilinea
To 5 in. (13 cm)

Vermilion Flycatcher
Pyrocephalus rubinus
To 6 in. (15 cm)

Yucatan Jay
Cyanocorax yucatanicus
To 14 in. (35 cm)

Tree Swallow
Tachycineta bicolor
To 6 in. (15 cm)

Brown Jay
Psilorhinus morio
To 16 in. (40 cm)
Juveniles have a yellow bill.

Social Flycatcher
Myiozetetes similis
To 6 in. (15 cm)

Green Jay
Cyanocorax yncas
To 11 in. (28 cm)

Great-tailed Grackle (Blackbird)
Quiscalus mexicanus
To 18 in. (45 cm)
Long tail is keel-shaped.

Montezuma's Oropendola
Psarocolius montezuma
To 20 in. (50 cm)
The similar chestnut-headed oropendola has a brown head and whitish bill.

Groove-billed Ani
Crotophaga sulcirostris
To 13 in. (33 cm)

Tropical Mockingbird
Mimus gilvus
To 10 in. (25 cm)

Gray Catbird
Dumetella carolinensis
To 9 in. (23 cm)
Note black cap and reddish undertail feathers.

Yellow-billed Cacique
Amblycercus holosericeus
To 10 in. (25 cm)

Red-winged Blackbird
Agelaius phoeniceus
To 9 in. (23 cm)

Yellow Warbler
Setophaga petechia
To 5 in. (13 cm)

Red-legged Honeycreeper
Cyanerpes cyaneus
To 5 in. (13 cm)

American Redstart
Setophaga ruticilla
To 5 in. (13 cm)

Magnolia Warbler
Setophaga magnolia
To 5 in. (13 cm)
Note large white wing patch.

Indigo Bunting
Passerina cyanea
To 6 in. (15 cm)

White-collared Seedeater
Sporophila torqueola
To 4.3 in. (11 cm)

Yellow-winged Tanager
Thraupis abbas
To 7 in. (18 cm)

Northern Cardinal
Cardinalis cardinalis
To 9 in. (23 cm)

Orchard Oriole
Icterus spurius
To 7 in. (18 cm)

Yellow-throated Euphonia
Euphonia hirundinacea
To 5 in. (13 cm)